The Crypto Renaissance

How Blockchain Art Markets are Disrupting the Traditional Gallery

Table of Contents

1. Introduction 1

2. The Rise of Crypto Art: An Overview 2

    2.1. The Genesis of Crypto Art 2

    2.2. The Eclosion of Digital Artistry 2

    2.3. The Disruption of Traditional Art Market 3

    2.4. The New Paradigm of Art Collecting 4

    2.5. The Upsurge of Crypto Art Marketplaces 4

    2.6. Navigating the Future of Crypto Art 5

3. Behind the Canvas: How Blockchain is Redefining Art 6

    3.1. The Catalytic Intersection of Art and Blockchain 6

    3.2. How Artists are Leveraging Blockchain 7

    3.3. Why Collectors are Embracing Blockchain 8

    3.4. Criticisms and Considerations 8

4. Disruptive Mavericks: Key Players in the Blockchain Art Market . 10

    4.1. The Tech Architects: Crypto Pioneers in the Art World 10

    4.2. The Artistic Alchemists: Trendsetting Crypto-Artists 11

    4.3. The Art Moguls: Influential Institutional Players 11

    4.4. The Critics and Curators: Thought Leaders in Blockchain
Art 12

    4.5. Dao Community: The Egalitarian Powerhouse 12

5. From Brush Strokes to Bytecode: The Creation of Digital Art 13

    5.1. The Digital Canvas 13

    5.2. The Concept of Reproduction 13

    5.3. Crypto-Art and Art Tokens 14

    5.4. Mass Distribution and Ownership. 15

    5.5. The Future of Art: Virtual Reality 15

6. The Virtual Gallery: Exploring Non-Fungible Tokens 17

    6.1. The Fundamentals of Non-Fungible Tokens 17

6.2. The Debut of NFTs into the Art Ecosystem 18

6.3. A Whole New Realm: Crypto Art Marketplaces 18

6.4. The Emergence of Virtual Galleries 19

6.5. The Controversy Around Environment Impact 19

6.6. Final Thoughts 20

7. Cryptoconomics and Art: An Unlikely, Yet Inevitable Marriage . . . 21

7.1. Understanding Crypto-Revolution in the Art Ecosystem 21

7.2. The Crypto-Economic Pulse of Art 22

7.3. Democratizing Art through Blockchain 22

7.4. Navigating Legal and Regulatory Hurdles 23

7.5. The Future of Art in the Age of Crypto-Economics 23

8. Brick-and-Mortar vs Digital: The Great Gallery Showdown 25

8.1. The Traditional Art Market 25

8.2. Enter Blockchain 26

8.3. The Influx of NFT Art 26

8.4. Monumental Highs and Significant Sales 27

8.5. Challenges and Critiques 27

8.6. Future Outlook: A Co-existence? 28

9. Investment in Crypto Art: Making Sense of Risk and Reward 29

9.1. Understanding Crypto Art 29

9.2. Assessing the Rewards 30

9.3. Framing the Risks 30

9.4. Navigating the Market: A Balanced Approach 31

10. Protecting Artists' Rights with Blockchain Technology 33

10.1. The Issue of Rights in the Digital Landscape 33

10.2. How Blockchain Can Protect Artists' Rights 34

10.3. Cases of Blockchain Usage in Protecting Artists' Rights . . . 34

10.4. Artists Going Direct to Market 35

10.5. In Conclusion: The Future of Artists' Rights 35

11. The Future of Fine Art: Crypto's Pioneering Influence 37

11.1. The Very Marriage: Traditional Fine Art and Cutting-Edge Technology ... 37

11.2. Cryptocurrency and the Transformation of Art Trade ... 38

11.3. Authenticity, Provenance, and the Blockchain Advantage ... 39

11.4. Tokenizing The Future: Benefits For Fine Art Collectors ... 39

11.5. The Roadblocks in the Journey ... 40

11.6. In Conclusion: A New Chapter Unveiled ... 40

Chapter 1. Introduction

Dive into the riveting world of digital revolution with our Special Report, "The Crypto Renaissance: How Blockchain Art Markets are Disrupting the Traditional Gallery". This comprehensive coverage melds finance, art, and technology into an engaging concoction. We craft a perfect blend of technical understanding and artistic flair, exploring the colossal shifts taking place in the world of art. Blockchain technology and cryptocurrencies have sparked an audacious new era, where traditional modes of art trade are being defiantly overhauled. Whether you're a tech enthusiast, an art lover, or an investor, this report unwraps the mysteries of the cutting-edge 'Crypto-Art' realm in a way that's accessible to all. Come, join us on this thrilling journey as we uncover the inspirations, the disruptors, the innovations, and the fascinating outcomes of this digital metamorphosis. This Special Report is more than just an investment for your mind; it's an investment in understanding the future.

Chapter 2. The Rise of Crypto Art: An Overview

Digital artistry and financial technology converged on an unprecedented scale with the advent of Crypto Art. The movement marks a significant departure from traditional art markets, creating a democratized platform for artists and collectors alike. Enabled by blockchain technology and fuelled by cryptocurrencies, this burgeoning sector faces relentless disruption, redefinition, and growth.

2.1. The Genesis of Crypto Art

The story of Crypto Art is intrinsically linked with blockchain technology - a distributed ledger system with unique properties that make it suitable for transparent and immutable records of transactions. Its first notable application was the cryptocurrency Bitcoin, introduced in 2008. However, while Bitcoin represented the dawn of digital currency, it is the Ethereum blockchain that sowed the seeds for Crypto Art, with its ability to attach a Non-Fungible Token (NFT) to a digital asset.

NFTs are unique digital tokens that can be attached to digital or real-world assets, giving them a provable identity and ownership on the blockchain. In the world of digital art, the creator mints an NFT as proof of authenticity and to enforce scarcity. This simple but effective mechanism heralded a new era of art trade, where art could be distributed freely while maintaining originality and value.

2.2. The Eclosion of Digital Artistry

The NFT evolution began modestly with CryptoPunks and CryptoKitties, simple pixel art and gaming token applications that started to reveal the potential value of NFTs. However, as more artists saw the revolutionary potential inherent to this technological feat, complex and inspiring digital artworks started to take shape. Artists worldwide, devoid of geographical constraints, began to create and present their art in this new, audacious domain.

Freed from physical constraints, digital artists embraced this medium to create visually stunning, multidimensional works that challenge traditional definitions of art. These art pieces are more than RGB values on a screen, they are storytelling mechanisms, encapsulating experiences and emotions into the digital realm. Whether it's 2D art, geometric sculptures or immersive virtual reality scenes, the tapestry of Crypto Art is as diverse as human creativity itself.

2.3. The Disruption of Traditional Art Market

While the digital format has allowed artists to push the boundaries of creativity, the use of blockchain technology and NFTs has fundamentally disrupted the traditional art market. Traditionally, artists have had to rely on galleries and auction houses to access a larger audience. These intermediaries often take a significant percentage of the profits, leaving artists with a diminished share of the earnings.

Crypto Art markets have knocked down these middlemen, enabling artists to sell their creations directly to the audience. This direct-to-consumer approach has led to greater earning potential for artists. Moreover, blockchain technology offers an immutable record of ownership and provenance of art pieces, instilling a newfound confidence in purchasing digital art which was often plagued by piracy and forgery concerns.

2.4. The New Paradigm of Art Collecting

Beyond democratising distribution and sales for artists, Crypto Art has brought seismic shifts to art collecting. The transparent nature of blockchain means every transaction involving a piece of Crypto Art is recorded permanently. This permanent ledger, visible to all, allows collectors to verify an art piece's history - a feature heavily valued in the realm of traditional art collecting where authenticity and rarity reign supreme.

Unlike physical art, NFTs can be easily transferred or traded worldwide without shipping or handling concerns. Crypto Art also opens up the realm of fractional ownership, allowing multiple collectors to own a 'share' of an artwork, broadening the scope of art investment.

Moreover, as Crypto Art enters the mainstream consciousness, collecting digital art has become about more than just the appreciation of talent and creativity. For many, it's about participating in a vibrant digital culture. Owning a Crypto Art piece can signify a badge of honor to showcase one's standing and influence within the virtual community.

2.5. The Upsurge of Crypto Art Marketplaces

The expansion of the Crypto Art universe has necessitated a new breed of marketplaces, specifically designed to handle the unique requirements of NFTs and digital art. Platforms like OpenSea, Rarible, and Foundation, among others, provide an interface for artists to mint and sell their NFTs. Meanwhile, collectors have a myriad of platforms where they can discover, bid, and purchase digital masterpieces.

These marketplaces also serve as social platforms, fostering communities of artists and collectors where ideas, appreciation, and criticisms are freely exchanged. Through these communal interactions, the relationship between the creator and the audience is reinforced, further underscoring the democratizing power of the Crypto Art revolution.

2.6. Navigating the Future of Crypto Art

While the world of Crypto Art is fascinating, it also treads in uncharted territory. The volatility of cryptocurrencies, the environmental impact of blockchain technology, the persistence of the initial hype—these are valid concerns that the sector must grapple with to secure its place in the future.

But one thing is evident. The digital revolution embodied by Crypto Art has turned the art world on its head. By fusing finance, technology, and creativity, it has given rise to a decentralized, democratized art market that is not only about commerce, but also about expression, identity, and community. In the grand narrative of art history, Crypto Art marks a pivotal chapter, championing the spirit of innovation and determination to challenge the status quo.

As each pixel finds its place, and each token is minted, the landscape of Crypto Art compels us to rethink, reimagine, and reinvent. It's not just about trading ink for pixels or canvases for screens—it's about embracing a new artistic paradigm, where creativity unfurls in the virtual realm, free from the shackles of the physical world. As we continue to witness this digital metamorphosis, one can't help but remain hooked to see what the next chapter holds for Crypto Art.

Chapter 3. Behind the Canvas: How Blockchain is Redefining Art

The art world has always been cyclical, filled with ebbs and flows of various movements and trends. With the advent of blockchain technology, a new cycle is beginning, slated to topple the power structures and the traditional mechanisms inherent within the art industry. Essentially, blockchain is a record-keeping method in which a list of data blocks is maintained by a peer-to-peer network. This technology is revolutionary in terms of its impact on the art market, not just from a transactional point of view but also fostering creativity and changing the creation process itself.

The dawn of this digital reinvention has born a new medium of art, popularly known as CryptoArt, which not only enables artists to take control of their work, but also to encapsulate proof of ownership, artist identity, and the origins of the artwork, combating the rampant issue of art fraud.

3.1. The Catalytic Intersection of Art and Blockchain

The art world and blockchain seem like unlikely allies. Yet, the commonality lies within their respective pursuit of ideations that question status quo. Blockchain's decentralized nature echoes the artist's quest for autonomy. While, the persistent issues of provenance, copyright, and authentication in the art world can find resolution through blockchain.

CryptoArt, often associated with Non-Fungible Tokens (NFTs), has revolutionized the creation, purchasing, and selling of art, challenging the traditional gatekeepers in the process. It allows artist's to tokenize their art pieces into digital assets, thereby ensuring a seamless integration of the creator's rights onto the blockchain. The tokenization process for art involves creating digital tokens on the blockchain, inherited with unique features that differentiate them from each other, allowing for individual valuation.

With an in-built contract functionality, CryptoArt paves the way for automated royalty payments each time the artwork is resold, establishing a continuous revenue stream for artists who previously faced a 'one-and-done' sales model. Through the simple application of smart contracts, the transaction gets cleaner, simpler, and transparent. This artist-centred revenue model stands in stark contrast to the traditional art market, which generally favors the intermediaries.

3.2. How Artists are Leveraging Blockchain

Artists around the globe are truly seizing this novel opportunity offered by blockchain. Renowned digital artist Mike Winkelmann, known as Beeple, made global headlines when his digital work "Everydays: The First 5000 Days" was sold as an NFT by Christie's auction house for a stunning $69 million. The sale not only marked a seismic shift in the art world but also underscored the immense opportunities that lie in the digital realm.

Artists can use blockchain to create a permanent, immutable record of their artwork, thereby addressing the issues of provenance and authenticity, which have long plagued the art world. Particularly, in terms of forgery and counterfeit art, blockchain's immutability presents a potential solution by establishing a secure, tamper-proof system of documenting and verifying the authenticity, thereby assuring potential buyers.

In a similar vein, artists now have the advantage of tracing their artwork, even after multiple sales, promoting better accountability and enabling them to collect royalties even from secondary sales through smart contracts. This considerably levels the playing field for artists, enabling them take charge of their art's journey from creation to transaction.

3.3. Why Collectors are Embracing Blockchain

Not only artists, but collectors too are increasingly enchanting towards blockchain technology. Blockchain's ability to provide transparent records of ownership history not only enhances trust, but also promises a clearer understanding of the art's origin and legitimacy. Collector's are now vouching for digitizing and tokenizing their collections to gain exposure and liquidity, challenging the previous limitations of physical possession and geographic barriers.

Moreover, fractional ownership is another intriguing blockchain prospect for art aficionados. Blockchain facilitates splitting a high-value artwork into numerous shares or tokens, allowing purchasers to own a fraction of the piece, a concept previously foreign to the art market. This opens doors for new breed of smaller investors, who hitherto could not afford to invest in highly priced works, democratizing access to the art world.

3.4. Criticisms and Considerations

While the horizon looks promising, the terrain of blockchain art is not without its controversies and concerns. Questions regarding the environmental impact have been prominently highlighted, especially considering the high energy usage of cryptocurrencies like Bitcoin. Additionally, the overall lack of regulation and the potential for market manipulation are concerning for many in these early stages.

Criticisms notwithstanding, the fusion of technology and artistry in the form of Blockchain Art carries significant potential. Offering an innovative solution for enduring issues in the art market, the power of blockchain technology is inspiring a new wave of artists and collectors, keen to explore this groundbreaking frontier that blends creativity, ownership, and financial potential.

As with every major movement, time will be the ultimate arbiter of success. The future might also see evolutions and adjustments in this model as it attempts to take on the broad spectrum of global art market's complexities. It is essential to continue the discourse on the opportunities and challenges brought on by this significant shift in the paradigm of art. For now, blockchain continues to redefine the canvas, bridging the traditional with the audaciously new.

Chapter 4. Disruptive Mavericks: Key Players in the Blockchain Art Market

Harnessing the might of blockchain, a cohort of revolutionary game-changers has risen to challenge the centuries-old system of the art world. This digital renaissance has mobilized a motley crew of tech wizards, avant-garde artists, and audacious investors who envision a democratized art marketplace shaped by digital tokens and blockchain.

4.1. The Tech Architects: Crypto Pioneers in the Art World

As influential as the artists themselves, the techno-scientific whizzes with their innovative abilities have emerged as the backbone of the blockchain art market. Powered by a shared dream, these individuals offer platforms that disrupt the traditional art market mechanics.

Among them, software engineer John Watkinson and entrepreneur Matt Hall headline this movement. After creating a collection of 10,000 unique pixelated faces known as CryptoPunks on the Ethereum blockchain, they attained unprecedented success in blockchain art. Their pioneer status finds validation in the $1.8 million sale of CryptoPunk 7804 in February 2021.

Other prominent names on the tech side include Matty Mo, the pseudonymous founder of "The Most Famous Artist" collective, and Vignesh Sundaresan, or Metakovan, who made headlines by purchasing Beeple's "Everydays: The First 5000 Days" for $69.3 million. These tech wizards, and many more, continue to redefine this nascent domain through their audacity, tech prowess, and vision.

4.2. The Artistic Alchemists: Trendsetting Crypto-Artists

Blockchain's influence has stirred a wave of avant-garde crypto-artists who defy convention with each artwork minted. Among them, digital artist Mike Winkelmann (better known as Beeple) dominates the industry. His digital behemoth mentioned earlier, "Everydays: The First 5000 Days," epitomizes the zeitgeist of the blockchain art world.

Two other incisive voices in crypto-art include Trevor Jones and PAK. Jones, a traditional painter turned crypto-artist, ups the game through his innovation 'NFT augmented reality art'. PAK, the anonymous entity, through his project "The Merge," auctioned 23,598 NFTs that struck a chord with the experimental undercurrent in crypto-art.

4.3. The Art Moguls: Influential Institutional Players

Driving the art sector towards blockchain inclusivity, auction houses and galleries have entered this fresh arena. Christie's and Sotheby's, two seasoned powerhouses, have enthusiastically auctioned off NFTs, fetching massive valuations.

NFT marketplace providers, such as OpenSea, SuperRare, and Rarible, have emerged as the eBay of digital assets. Their proliferating platforms engender a thriving ecosystem for creators and collectors alike, thereby advancing blockchain art.

OpenSea, with its distinctive approach of hosting all types of NFTs, captures the variety in crypto-art. SuperRare, on the other hand, emphasizes selectivity with a focus on curated, single-edition digital artworks.

4.4. The Critics and Curators: Thought Leaders in Blockchain Art

Crypto-art is scrutinized, critiqued, and venerated by a fresh breed of critics and curators who breathe life into this space. They provide intellectual richness to the crypto-art conversation. Jason Bailey, the founder of Artnome, provides rich analyses and opinion pieces on the current trends. Jessica Angel, a visual artist and crypto-enthusiast, curates in-depth resources for the crypto art community.

4.5. Dao Community: The Egalitarian Powerhouse

Also crucial in this ecosystem are Decentralized Autonomous Organizations (DAO), where each member has a say in managing collected artworks. DAOs like Flamingo DAO and PleasrDAO merit mention for their democratic model and significant purchases of high-ticket digital art.

Blockchain has woven an exciting network of tech architects, artists, critiques, and investors to re-imagine the art world. Through a shared ambition, they sustain an ethos of inclusivity, transparency, and democratization, positioning the blockchain art market as an agent of revitalization within the art scene. Their collective action challenges and disrupts the traditional modes of operation, giving rise to a mercurial art movement with the strength to defy the past and shape the future.

Chapter 5. From Brush Strokes to Bytecode: The Creation of Digital Art

The digitization of art is not just a mere transferal of creative processes onto a digital platform. It is a revolution that has transformed art's very essence, from its creation to distribution and ownership.

5.1. The Digital Canvas

Instead of brushes and paints, the digital artist uses computer software as instruments and pixel grids as their canvas. Artists often employ advanced software and hardware like Photoshop, Illustrator, digital tablets, and styluses to bring their pieces to life. Some of these tools even mimic the feel of traditional art techniques so succinctly that transitioning artists find a sense of familiarity. There's an inescapable immediacy, a sensation of the brush moving across the screen and making a direct impact on the image; a feature that traditional tools cannot replicate.

Beyond the basic tools, digital art software often comes with extensive sets of features like layers, filters, effects, and transformation tools; which can manipulate the artwork in ways that are almost impossible to achieve in traditional art. The power of these tools in the right hands can create unprecedented art forms, a blend of the illustrative and the experimental, pushing boundaries of aesthetics and ideas.

5.2. The Concept of Reproduction

Reproduction of art has been a contentious issue since the advent of technology that allowed mass reproduction. The issue of originality becomes confusing when reproductions are indistinguishable from the original piece. But digital art has subverted this debate by essentially being immune to the issues that plague physical art. The digital form allows artists to create pieces that are fundamentally multi-original.

Every copy of a digital artwork is a perfect and complete version of the original, identical down to each pixel. The nature of digital art has taken away the power of the original; the Mona Lisa's price may diminish if there were a thousand identical versions, but a digital piece's value is not affected by replication due to its inherent nature.

5.3. Crypto-Art and Art Tokens

The intrinsic reproducibility and distributability of digital art have left it vulnerable to theft, forgery, and uncontrolled distribution. However, with novel cryptographic technologies like blockchain, digital artists now have the ability to control duplication, ownership, and traceability of their work. Crypto-art refers to digital artwork linked to a token on a blockchain, which authenticates the art's originality and provides proof of ownership.

Crypto-art has a dual existence - the art piece itself and its representative token on the blockchain. This token, known as an art token or NFT (Non Fungible Token), contains details about the artwork, the artist, and change of ownership. The token is unique and cannot be replicated or replaced, unlike the artwork it represents. The ownership of the token correlates to the ownership of the associated art piece, making it a powerful tool against forgery and theft.

5.4. Mass Distribution and Ownership.

The decentralization ethos that underpins the blockchain mechanism fundamentally alters the dynamics of art consumption and ownership. It refines the relationship between creators and consumers, making the market more open, equitable, and democratic.

The blockchain, with its P2P network, deregulates the art world by eliminating intermediaries like galleries and auction houses. Artists can now directly mint, price, and sell their artworks to the global audience. It has also intensified the discourse on fractional ownership, which refers to the concept wherein multiple individuals can invest in and collectively own expensive works of art.

This democratization of the art market, in turn, has fuelled new trends like social value investing, which is changing the way people interact with art while providing artists with new avenues to express their creativity and build financial stability.

5.5. The Future of Art: Virtual Reality

As we further move towards the completive digitization of art, the prospects of virtual and augmented reality emerge as new frontiers for artists to explore. Using VR technology, artists can create immersive, multi-sensory experiences that dwarf the two-dimensional constraints of physical and digital canvas.

Art viewings have also shifted to digital spaces. Blockchain technology powers digital art marketplaces and virtual galleries, where patrons can buy, sell, and display art by merely owning their respective NFTs.

With these advancements, it isn't fantastical to predict that future museums may exist only in the virtual realm, with each visitor experiencing art in their private, immersive spaces.

From brush strokes on canvas to bytes on a computer, digital art is continually transforming the way artists create and the way consumers interact with art. This shift constitutes more than a change in medium. It's a revelation of what art can be. With no signs of slowing down, this digital revolution promises a future where art is more accessible, inclusive, and influential than ever before.

Chapter 6. The Virtual Gallery: Exploring Non-Fungible Tokens

Oftentimes, while wading through the depths of blockchain technology and the ambiguous realm of cryptocurrencies, we tend to forget a derivative of this novel tech that is ceaselessly redefining and reshaping the world of digitized art: Non-Fungible Tokens (NFTs). An essential tenet of the genesis known as 'Crypto-Art,' NFTs have undeniably imposed a disruptive force on the conventional gallery setting.

6.1. The Fundamentals of Non-Fungible Tokens

Non-Fungible Tokens (NFTs), in simple terms, are unique cryptographic tokens that exist on a blockchain. Unlike cryptocurrencies such as Bitcoin or Ethereum, which are 'fungible' by design and can be exchanged on a one-for-one basis, NFTs are inherently unique – each token carries distinct information that sets it apart from any other token.

Analogously, consider a painting. No matter how intricately a replica may be created, it can never carry the same aura, the stories, the brush strokes, and the variations in color that the original accommodates. This uniqueness and irreplicability, when translated into the digital world, vest into NFTs.

By leveraging the decentralized aspects of blockchain technology, NFTs manage to tokenize everything from digital art and music to virtual real estate, and even tweets. Each NFT has metadata associated with it, which is essentially a digital certificate of authenticity verifying its originality and ownership.

6.2. The Debut of NFTs into the Art Ecosystem

NFTs, although a recent addition to the art marketplace, have redefined the concept of buying and owning art. Traditional art marketplaces often include many intermediaries, including art galleries, agents, and auction houses, among other things. NFTs, on the other hand, are predominantly traded on digital marketplaces, allowing artists to sell their work directly to consumers.

Through this direct-to-consumer model, artists retain more control over their work and capture a larger percentage of sales. Furthermore, unlike traditional art sales, the artist continues to earn with each subsequent sale of the artwork. Such a profit-sharing model is made possible by implementing smart contract technology that automatically redistributes a portion of each resale back to the original creator.

6.3. A Whole New Realm: Crypto Art Marketplaces

Marketplaces such as OpenSea, Rarible, and Foundation have played an instrumental role in the rise and proliferation of 'crypto art.' These platforms offer an interactive interface to facilitate the buying, selling, and trading of NFTs. A stark departure from hushed, art gallery auctions, these platforms create an environment that encourages creators, potential buyers, and curious onlookers to interact.

There's also an element of gamification involved. Many platforms reward the most active users with 'platform tokens,' which can in turn be used to vote for platform upgrades or collectible drops, thereby further intensifying the overall marketplace experience. This method is embraced because it strives to blur the strict societal line separating 'art' from 'entertainment' which is often prevalent in traditional gallery setups.

6.4. The Emergence of Virtual Galleries

With the advent of virtual reality and a surge in remotely-conducted activities in response to the ongoing pandemic, virtual galleries have emerged as the new-age showcase for art pieces minted as NFTs.

Notably, platforms such as Decentraland and CryptoVoxels have committed to creating virtual 'parcel-based' worlds, where users can buy, sell, and build upon virtual land. These platforms engage users in a 3D, immersive experience, where they can discover and purchase NFTs displayed in a variety of virtual structures such as museums, galleries, and sculptures.

Imagine the surreal experience of stepping into an entirely different realm — an alternate universe, if you will — where every wall, every structure, is adorned with the radiant beauty of countless artworks, each more captivating than the last. This is the charming allure of virtual galleries.

6.5. The Controversy Around Environment Impact

Despite the potential and exuberance, NFTs are not without controversy. Art created and sold as NFTs often require intense computational resources. The process known as 'minting' — where digital art is converted into an NFT and added to the blockchain — is energy-intensive. This has led to concerns about the carbon footprint of the NFT ecosystem.

While this is a significant concern, it is worthwhile to note that many NFT platforms and blockchain networks are exploring ways to address this challenge. As a part of moving towards a 'proof of stake' consensus mechanism, Ethereum, the most widely-used blockchain for NFT transactions, is striving to drastically reduce its carbon footprint.

6.6. Final Thoughts

As we step into this new era of digital art, the advent of NFTs signifies a shift in how we create, buy, sell, and perceive art. The virtual gallery, proliferated by these unique digital tokens, is challenging the traditional norms and enhancing the accessibility and interactivity of the art world.

Indeed, the 'Crypto Art Revolution,' powered by NFTs, is pushing us to reconsider our understanding of value and ownership in the digital age. Whether this revolution will democratize art or turn it into a speculative market remains uncertain. What is definite, though, is that we are witnessing the dawn of a new artistic epoch, one that is audaciously rewriting the rules and norms of the traditional gallery. This monumental shift, dear reader, is truly the heart of our 'Crypto Renaissance.'

Chapter 7. Cryptoconomics and Art: An Unlikely, Yet Inevitable Marriage

In the dawn of the 21st century, the world was introduced to blockchain technology and cryptocurrencies, potent tools that have since initiated a ripple effect across various sectors, from finance to healthcare, and, more recently, art. As unlikely as the pairing may seem, the marriage of crypto-economics and the art world harbors immense transformative potential, empowering artists and disrupting traditional art markets.

7.1. Understanding Crypto-Revolution in the Art Ecosystem

Blockchain art, often referred to as Crypto Art, is digital art related to blockchain technology or that exists on the blockchain in the form of Non-Fungible Tokens (NFTs). This form of art has redefined artistic creation, ownership, and monetization, marking a significant shift from the conventional methods facilitated by physical galleries and art dealers.

An essential aspect of crypto art is the notion of digital ownership. The incorruptible security and decentralization offered by blockchain technology authenticate the digital ownership of art, preserving the uniqueness of the art piece and establishing the creator's originality. This is a stark departure from traditional digital art, which suffers from a lack of authenticated ownership due to unrestricted copying and sharing.

7.2. The Crypto-Economic Pulse of Art

Crypto-economic models, underlying this sphere of Digital Art, infuse the creative process with an economic structure that encourages more equitable systems and novel investment opportunities. It's essential to appreciate the invaluable role played by crypto-economics in the emergence and evolution of blockchain art markets.

An artist, traditionally reliant on galleries and dealers, can now mint a digital artwork as an NFT directly onto the blockchain, retaining the entirety of the sales proceeds as well as the potential to earn royalties from future transactions of that particular artwork.

Collectors and investors, bypassing auction houses or galleries, can buy artwork directly from creators or previous owners online. Blockchain transparency, along with the indelible nature of each transaction recorded, inspires confidence in the market participants, minimizing the risk of forgeries or double-sales.

7.3. Democratizing Art through Blockchain

The intrinsic features of blockchain technology — decentralization, transparency, and security — synergize to democratize the art world. The democratizing effect is manifold: it opens the art market to global participants, it democratizes wealth creation by allowing artists to participate in the financial success of their work, and it promotes an egalitarian system where anyone can create, buy, or sell art.

In conventional art markets, the transaction fees and costs associated with intermediaries such as galleries or auction houses often sideline independent artists and emerging collectors. However, blockchain art platforms, by eliminating these intermediaries, enable a more accessible and affordable art trading ecosystem.

The open access nature of blockchain also provides artists from more impoverished parts or those previously unrecognized in the art world, an equal podium to showcase their work to a global audience.

7.4. Navigating Legal and Regulatory Hurdles

Despite the profound potential that blockchain art markets offer, they do not exist in a vacuum. The legal and regulatory landscape associated with cryptocurrencies and blockchain technology remains complex, varying widely across different jurisdictions.

Artists and collectors must navigate these uncertainties while participating in blockchain art markets, such as those around copyright infringement, tax obligations, or even privacy considerations in the context of public transaction records.

Both artists and collectors must be cautious and informed about their rights and obligations under their respective jurisdictions. To ensure legality while engaging in blockchain art transactions, consulting with a lawyer well-versed in the intersection of blockchain, art, and the law is prudent.

7.5. The Future of Art in the Age of Crypto-Economics

The application of crypto-economics in the art world signifies a step into uncharted territory. This technology instigates a re-evaluation of our current systems and calls for transformation.

In the near future, we can envisage an even more extensive adoption of blockchain in the art world, with physical art being tagged to NFTs, thus ensuring their provenance. We can also expect innovative forms of artistic collaboration or co-creation facilitated by the inherent structure of NFTs and smart contracts.

Indeed, we are on the precipice of a digital renaissance, with Crypto Art forming the vanguard of an audacious new era. The union of crypto-economics and art, though unlikely initially, spells an inevitable shift, heralding a more democratic, equitable, and vibrant world of art.

Chapter 8. Brick-and-Mortar vs Digital: The Great Gallery Showdown

Boasting centuries of history, brick-and-mortar art galleries have dominated the scene, bringing countless artists to prominence and holding high the beacon of expression, culture, and refinement. Nevertheless, the advent of digital technology, coupled with the rise of cryptocurrencies and blockchain, is challenging the status quo to its very core. This new paradigm offers entrance to the world of art to audiences, creators, and investors alike, rendering geographical and financial boundaries obsolete.

8.1. The Traditional Art Market

The traditional art market has existed for centuries, with brick-and-mortar galleries and auction houses serving as the epicenters of trade. The market operates on trust, provenance, historical pricing, and an artist's reputation. At its core, this world highly values and promotes the physical presence and authenticity of an artwork. Art enthusiasts and potential investors flock to meticulously-curated exhibitions, finding esoteric connection with heartfelt expressions and indelible strokes of the human condition.

It is a world of exclusivity, governed by gatekeepers who decide which artists and pieces get shown, and at what price. Much of this decision-making process is influenced by an artist's existing reputation, schooling, awards, previous exhibitions and critical acclaim. For emerging artists, it can be an uphill battle to gain recognition and appreciation. Moreover, the sheer logistics of displaying and selling physical art necessitates significant overhead costs concerning storage, insurance, and shipping.

8.2. Enter Blockchain

With the rise of digital technology, blockchain, and cryptocurrencies, a cyberspace upheaval has been incited within the art market. In digitizing the trading process and harnessing the power of decentralization, blockchain technology presents a disruptive force in the art world, directly confronting the traditional market.

Blockchain-based digital art markets, also known as Non-Fungible Tokens (NFTs), aim to dissolve geographical borders and personal bias, encouraging artists of all styles, experience, and backgrounds to showcase their artwork. Essentially, blockchain is a public ledger, recording transactions that are not only decentralized but also transparent, immutable, and secure. Each piece of art is transformed into a unique digital asset, irreplicable and indisputably owned by its purchaser.

8.3. The Influx of NFT Art

One of the most significant shifts in the art market has been the rise of Non-Fungible Tokens (NFTs). These digital assets are unique pieces of art, stored on a blockchain, and each has a specific value based on its originality and the artist's reputation. The rise of NFTs has disrupted the traditional art market by allowing artists to sell their works directly to consumers, without the need for an intermediary like a gallery or auction house.

These pieces of digital art are bought and sold in a market that, like cryptocurrencies, is open and operates 24/7. This implies no time-zone restrictions and guarantees an uninterrupted trading process, unheard of in traditional gallery dealings. Moreover, costs relating to logistics and storage are virtually non-existent in the digital art market, providing a cost-effective avenue for both artists and collectors.

One prominent attraction of NFT art is the benefit it serves to emerging artists. In the fiercely competitive traditional art market, talented new painters, sculptors, and illustrators often struggle to break through. With NFTs, these digital artists can bypass many barriers to entry, gain rapid recognition, and draw sizable income from their work.

8.4. Monumental Highs and Significant Sales

Art sales fueled by blockchain technology have witnessed astronomical highs recently. The most notable, a digital-only artwork by the artist Beeple, sold for a staggering $69.3 million at Christie's, a figure previously unthinkable in the digital art world. This event sent waves through the entire art industry, signaling a shift in perception of what art could be, how it could be traded, and its potential worth.

It's not just the highest echelons of art sales that blockchain is influencing. Across the board, artists are finding value in tokenizing their work, and collectors are seeing the potential for investment within digital art. With much of these transactions taking place directly between artists and collectors, the price bump afforded by commissions to middlemen is often avoided, meaning that digital art can be both more profitable for the artist and more affordable for the buyer.

8.5. Challenges and Critiques

Like all disruptive innovation, the digital transformation of the art market is met with critiques and challenges. Fraud, copyright infringement, and excessive energy consumption are concerns raised in the blockchain art market, similar to concerns in the wider blockchain and cryptocurrency sphere. Furthermore, the highly volatile nature of the blockchain market creates an unstable environment for both artists and collectors alike.

Another critique is the lacking tangibility of digital art; physicality holds an irreplaceable allure for many art enthusiasts, one that a digital jpg simply can't emulate. The traditional art market will always provide an emotive, tactile experience that offers enrichment in a way digital art couldn't cater to.

8.6. Future Outlook: A Co-existence?

The onset of digital disruption within the art market signifies a significant transformation, much like the movement from physical letters to digital communication. However, one might argue the difference lies in art's deeply personal and emotional appreciation, challenging the complete digitization of the art market in exclusive terms.

By providing artists with an accessible platform and revolutionizing art trade methods, blockchain markets surely hold a definite place within the future art scene. However, the tangible allure of physical art is likely to remain a critical part of human artistic expression. The two realms could coexist, offering complementary avenues for the appreciation and trade of art – each with their unique attractions, constraints, and market dynamics.

In conclusion, the blockchain revolution in art isn't a definitive pivot from the traditional. Instead, it's the addition of a new layer that may well serve a new demographic of artists and audience, thriving symbiotically and shaping the future of art and cultural expression altogether.

Chapter 9. Investment in Crypto Art: Making Sense of Risk and Reward

As we dip our toes into a fascinating new world of artistry laced with technology, it's pivotal to understand, at its core, the financial implications associated with crypto-art; most notably, the risk and reward balance. Crypto art, also known as NFT art, has enjoyed an explosive rise in popularity and has proven lucrative for both artists and investors alike. Yet, like any burgeoning market, it's also fraught with uncertainty and volatility. With that in mind, we'll scrutinize this invigorating territory, aiming to provide clear insights into risk management and the potential rewards on offer.

9.1. Understanding Crypto Art

Crypto art, or NFT art, named after the Non-Fungible Tokens (NFT) it employs, is a type of digital art associated with blockchain technology. Unlike cryptocurrencies such as Bitcoin or Ethereum that are fungible and can be exchanged on a like-for-like basis, NFTs are unique or 'non-fungible'. This uniqueness introduces rarity into the digital space, a characteristic that's fundamental to the concept of art's value.

The blockchain's immutable ledger technology enables these digital artworks to retain proof of authenticity and ownership - information that, in the physical art world, is represented by a certificate of authenticity. In essence, this technology liberates art from the limitations of physicality - no need for storage, no fear of damage, loss, or theft, and seamless, cost-effective global transactions.

9.2. Assessing the Rewards

The world of Crypto art offers a wealth of potential rewards, those of which can be jotted down as follows:

1. Lower Entry Threshold: Unlike traditional art markets, the crypto art space is easily accessible to artists and investors globally, regardless of status or geographic location. One enduring beauty of the blockchain is its inherent democratisation of resources.

2. Royalties on Secondary Sales: Smart contracts associated with NFT allow artists to receive royalties every time their work is resold. The traditional art market hasn't offered this benefit, meaning artists profit only from the initial sale.

3. High Returns on Investment: The crypto-art market has registered explosive growth. In March 2021, the artist Mike Winkelmann, popularly known as Beeple, sold an NFT art piece 'Everydays: The First 5000 Days' at Christie's auction for a staggering $69 million.

4. Digital Ownership: The purchaser of a crypto art piece becomes the authorised digital owner—something that can be proven beyond doubt because of the blockchain storage of this data. This system establishes a unique connection between the artist and the collector.

9.3. Framing the Risks

However, as with every silver-lined reward, there are substantial risks tangled in this digital revolution.

1. Market Volatility: The NFT market has proven to be highly volatile - a factor that can be attributed to its nascent state and quick-burgeoning interest.

2. Uncertain Regulatory Environment: The laws and regulations

around crypto art remain ill-defined, primarily as the legislation tries to catch up with the pace at which the technology is evolving.

3. Connection to Cryptocurrency: As the NFT market is predominantly conducted in cryptocurrencies, it shares the risks associated with them - including potential hacking, lack of consumer protection, and the aforementioned price volatility.

4. High Energy Consumption: NFT transactions require a lot of computational power and, therefore, consume substantial energy. This high energy consumption leads to a significant environmental footprint - a factor that has stirred outspoken criticism.

5. Intellectual Property Concerns: While blockchain's immutability offers a new definition of ownership, it doesn't stop unauthorized duplication of digital images, leading to disputes around copyright and intellectual property.

9.4. Navigating the Market: A Balanced Approach

Considering the hefty rewards and accompanying risks, it's clear that a balanced, strategic approach is necessary when venturing into the world of crypto art investment. Understanding, research, prudence, and a touch of boldness are crucial for success - the same ingredients that are key to any traditional investment portfolio.

Crypto art is challenging norms and rewriting the rule book on art's creation, distribution, and ownership. Investing in this space is not merely transactional; it's about nurturing a new paradigm, a paradigm where art and technology coalesce, creating an extraordinary, vibrant market that's still unfolding. It's about being part of something transformative and having a stake in the future of art in itself. For those who dare to explore, it's a thrilling journey of discovery and truly bold capital allocation.

Chapter 10. Protecting Artists' Rights with Blockchain Technology

The movement from traditional art to digital has primarily been marked by a rapid expansion of the art industry into the technological space. Yet, unfortunately, this has resulted in a sea of uncertainties surrounding the protection of artist's rights. In the physical art world, the artist's touch - the singularity of each piece, its texture, its definite presence, commands great value. In the digital space, however, the ease of reproduction creates a challenge. Blockchain technology, providing new ways to verify, protect, and trade art, appears to be a promising solution to this predicament.

10.1. The Issue of Rights in the Digital Landscape

With the rapid evolution of technology and the rise of digital art, artists have been tasked with the daunting challenge of protecting their work. In the physical art world, this is relatively straightforward - physical paintings or sculptures are harder to duplicate, and the rarity often contributes to their value. Digital art, however, is almost effortless to reproduce perfectly. This has long been a problem with digital content in general - how does one maintain rights over something that can be flawlessly copied in a matter of seconds?

The traditional answer has depended on laws and regulations — copyright laws. But these laws can be difficult to enforce, especially in today's Internet age. Blockchain technology has the potential to offer a practical alternative to this problem, and it's all about authenticity, ownership, and traceability.

10.2. How Blockchain Can Protect Artists' Rights

A blockchain is a decentralized and distributed digital ledger that records transactions across many computers in such a way that previous transactions cannot be altered retroactively. Blockchain's intrinsic properties - decentralization, transparency, and immutability - make it an ideal tool for artists seeking to protect their work.

Blockchain technology allows artists to register their work within a secure system. This registered piece of artwork then becomes attached to an immutable, transparent chain of ownership. It also provides proof of authenticity and originality, which can be extremely difficult to provide in the digital art world.

Ownership details, including the creator's name, the date of creation, its price history, and the current owner, are stored in a secure and auditable way. Artists can now provide an indelible proof of their work's origin, and potential buyers can trace ownership back to the artist's original creation, discouraging theft and unauthorized reproduction.

10.3. Cases of Blockchain Usage in Protecting Artists' Rights

Several platforms have begun using blockchain technology to create a secure, transparent marketplace for digital art. One example is Artory, a blockchain-based art registry. This platform uses blockchain to create a trusted, tamper-proof record of an artwork's history. This includes a record of transfers of ownership, exhibitions, restorations, and even theft.

Another platform, Codex, provides an anonymous, encrypted ledger for artwork and collectibles. Artists, collectors, and auction houses can record an object's identity, provenance, and transactions, thereby ensuring its authenticity and ownership history.

Platforms like these are helping to bolster the value of digital art by providing a secure means of verifying their authenticity and protecting artists' rights. By creating a reputable ownership history for each piece, they're fortifying the digital art industry against theft, forgery, and disputes.

10.4. Artists Going Direct to Market

Blockchain technology not only protects the rights of digital artists, but it also enables them to bypass the traditional art industry and sell directly to collectors. Thanks to blockchain-enabled marketplaces, artists can tokenize their artwork, creating a digital certificate of ownership that can be sold and traded. This enables artists to monetize their work more effectively and retain a greater share of their work's value.

Many blockchain art platforms offer this functionality. For instance, platforms like OpenSea and Rarible allow artists to mint unique non-fungible tokens (NFTs) for their work, which are then sold or auctioned to collectors. These platforms not only offer a marketplace but also create a public ledger of an art piece's ownership history, deterring counterfeit and fraud.

10.5. In Conclusion: The Future of Artists' Rights

It's clear that blockchain offers valuable solutions for artists' rights protection. By providing an unalterable digital ledger of each artwork's history, it helps establish provenance, confirm authenticity, and deter unauthorized reproductions. Moreover, by tokenizing digital art, artists can directly sell their works, breaking free of the constraints of the traditional art market.

However, these solutions are still in their early stages, and many challenges loom ahead. Legal frameworks for blockchain and NFTs are still underdeveloped. Issues concerning intellectual property rights within the cryptographic space continue to be contentious. Despite these uncertainties, blockchain technology undoubtedly holds great promise. It can revolutionize the art world, ensuring artist's rights protection along with the rise of the digital art market.

As artists and collectors embrace this technology, the next few years will be crucial in shaping the future of artists' rights. This wave has only just begun, and its potential impact on artists, collectors, and the art industry at large remains to be seen.

Chapter 11. The Future of Fine Art: Crypto's Pioneering Influence

The world of art is in the midst of a remarkable digital transformation. An audacious new era that uniquely fuses finance, fine art, and cutting-edge technology is on the horizon; its key accelerant being blockchain and cryptocurrency technology. This undeniable marriage of art and technology is causing colossal shifts in the dynamics of how fine art is preserved, bought, sold, authenticated, and undoubtedly appreciated.

11.1. The Very Marriage: Traditional Fine Art and Cutting-Edge Technology

Traditional fine art, the paragon of classic cultural expression, may seem an unlikely bedfellow with modern blockchain technology. To fully appreciate this intriguing chemistry, it is paramount to understand the concept of digital representation of assets.

Blockchain acts as an immutable ledger, recording transactions in blocks that are mathematically linked to one another, creating an unbroken chain of historical record. The rise of blockchain's derived application, known as the non-fungible token (NFT), facilitates the association of digital art with a unique, non-transferable blockchain entry. By using NFTs, artworks become digital assets, capable of being 'minted', sold, and resold, offering promising new layers of flexibility, accessibility, and assurance for artists and collectors alike.

In the digital art realm, when an artwork is 'minted', a new NFT is created. This NFT, a sort of 'digital certificate of authenticity', is linked permanently to that particular piece of art. This inherent link creates immense value for digital assets, allowing them to exist independently in the virtual realm, yet retain objective value much like their physical counterparts.

11.2. Cryptocurrency and the Transformation of Art Trade

The decentralized nature of blockchain technology and cryptocurrencies presents an exciting opportunity to make the fine art market more accessible and democratic. Decentralization opens avenues for artists to essentially cut out the middleman – such as auction houses or galleries – allowing them to sell their art directly to collectors. While controversial, this is a notable advantage for artists, particularly those who find it difficult to break into the traditional gallery system.

Blockchain-based platforms empower artists with the freedom to control the pricing of their work, as well as the ability to design secondary sales royalties into their digital contracts. This means that artists can potentially continue to benefit financially from the escalating value of their work on the secondary market – a privilege that has traditionally eluded most artists in the existing art economy.

Moreover, the integration of cryptocurrency payments into the art market can facilitate a global reach, transcending physical borders and enabling cross-border transactions with remarkable ease. Such democratization could herald a new age of diversified participation in the fine art market, attracting a wider spectrum of buyers and sellers.

11.3. Authenticity, Provenance, and the Blockchain Advantage

One of the most significant values offered by blockchain technology in the art world is its potential to solve the perennial issue of provenance and authenticity. Each transaction made on the blockchain is transparent and traceable. Given the immutable nature of the blockchain ledger, the origin and movement of an artwork can be traced back to its inception.

This transparency offers reassurance to buyers and reduces the risk of fraud, forgeries, and illegal trafficking of artworks. By creating an irrefutable chain of title, blockchain offers a compelling answer to historical concerns surrounding counterfeit art. A clear-cut, transparent trail of ownership infuses unprecedented confidence in the art trade.

11.4. Tokenizing The Future: Benefits For Fine Art Collectors

The advent of blockchain technology and cryptocurrencies offers a slew of advantages for collectors. The ability to fractionalize ownership through tokenization in the digital art realm could potentially deliver unmatched liquidity to the art market. Shared ownership allows art lovers and investors to buy a fraction of an artwork, even if they can't afford the entire piece. This fractional ownership could then be easily traded on various platforms.

Moreover, the crypto-art market operates around the clock, meaning buyers and sellers from different time zones can strike deals in real-time, a feature that bypasses the traditional restrictions of opening hours in galleries or auction houses.

11.5. The Roadblocks in the Journey

While blockchain technology has immense potential to revolutionize the world of fine art, notable barriers need to be overcome. These include environmental concerns related to the excessive energy usage of blockchain networks, the volatility of cryptocurrency, and the topic of intellectual property rights in the digital realm.

Furthermore, resistance from the established art community could pose significant challenges. Change is invariably met with skepticism, particularly when it threatens existing power structures. The traditional art world may not immediately embrace this change, and it remains to be seen how it will adjust to these extraordinary digital innovations.

11.6. In Conclusion: A New Chapter Unveiled

On the cusp of a digital revolution, the intersection of fine art and cryptocurrency is reshaping the future of art creation, curation, collection, and trade in unforeseen ways. As we move forward into this digital metamorphosis, there are uncertainties, confusions, and resistance, but there is also enormous potential. As blockchain technology continues to evolve and reshape the landscape for artists, collectors, and investors, one thing is clear: the enchanting drama of the 'Crypto-Art' realm is just beginning. The revolution promises to ensure the inclusivity and democratization of the art world, blending traditional charm with unequivocal innovation. The future of fine art, influenced by the pioneering leap of crypto and blockchain, certainly promises a remarkable spectacle.